CANYON JOURNEY

JUDITH WILKINSON

ARTWORK BY DITTY DOORNBOS

Shoestring Press

Printed by imprintdigital
Upton Pyne, Exeter
www.imprintdigital.com

Typeset by narrator
www.narrator.me.uk
info@narrator.me.uk
033 022 300 39

Published by Shoestring Press
19 Devonshire Avenue, Beeston, Nottingham, NG9 1BS
(0115) 925 1827
www.shoestringpress.co.uk

First published 2016

For the drawings Ditty Doornbos used pencils and coloured chalk
Photographer of the paintings: Michael Wilkinson
Photograph of author and illustrator by Patrick Reyskens

ISBN 978-1-910323-53-3

CANYON JOURNEY

ACKNOWLEDGEMENTS

Poems included in this chapbook were first published, in slightly different versions, in: *Acumen* and *De Hoffeskrant*.

NOTE

This sequence was inspired by the drawings, journals and letters of Ditty Doornbos, in which she documents her journey through chronic illness. Ditty kindly gave me access to her artwork and journals, and with this wealth of material to draw on, the poems gradually took shape, in close consultation with Ditty.

This book is dedicated to our parents:

Han Wilkinson-Dekhuijzen and the late David Wilkinson

and

the late Ans Himpers and Joop Doornbos

CONTENTS

1 Heading Down 1
2 Stuck 3
3 Still-life 5
4 You 7
5 Too Early 9
6 Daytime Nightmare 11
7 Nadir 13
8 Walking 15
9 Love 17
10 Relapse 19
11 The Oldest Dream 21
12 Threshold 25
13 Staying 27

1 HEADING DOWN

'I dreamt I'd fallen into an ancient desert canyon. Its walls
towered over me.' – Ditty Doornbos

I can still distinguish sounds up there,
on the distant ledges of this canyon,
people beckoning towards the limitless sky,
the logic of horizons,
but this shaft is too deep,
the walls too slippery
and I lack rope, gear, skill.

If I am to travel further downwards,
let it be with my eyes open, pen and pencil in hand,
so I can record this time in the desert –
dream time, nightmare time –
however trivial in the scheme of things,
however tortuous, offbeat,
encompassing

and let me come back,
some better prepared hour,
to the land of the beckoning living,
to the beautiful customs of every day

and report my findings

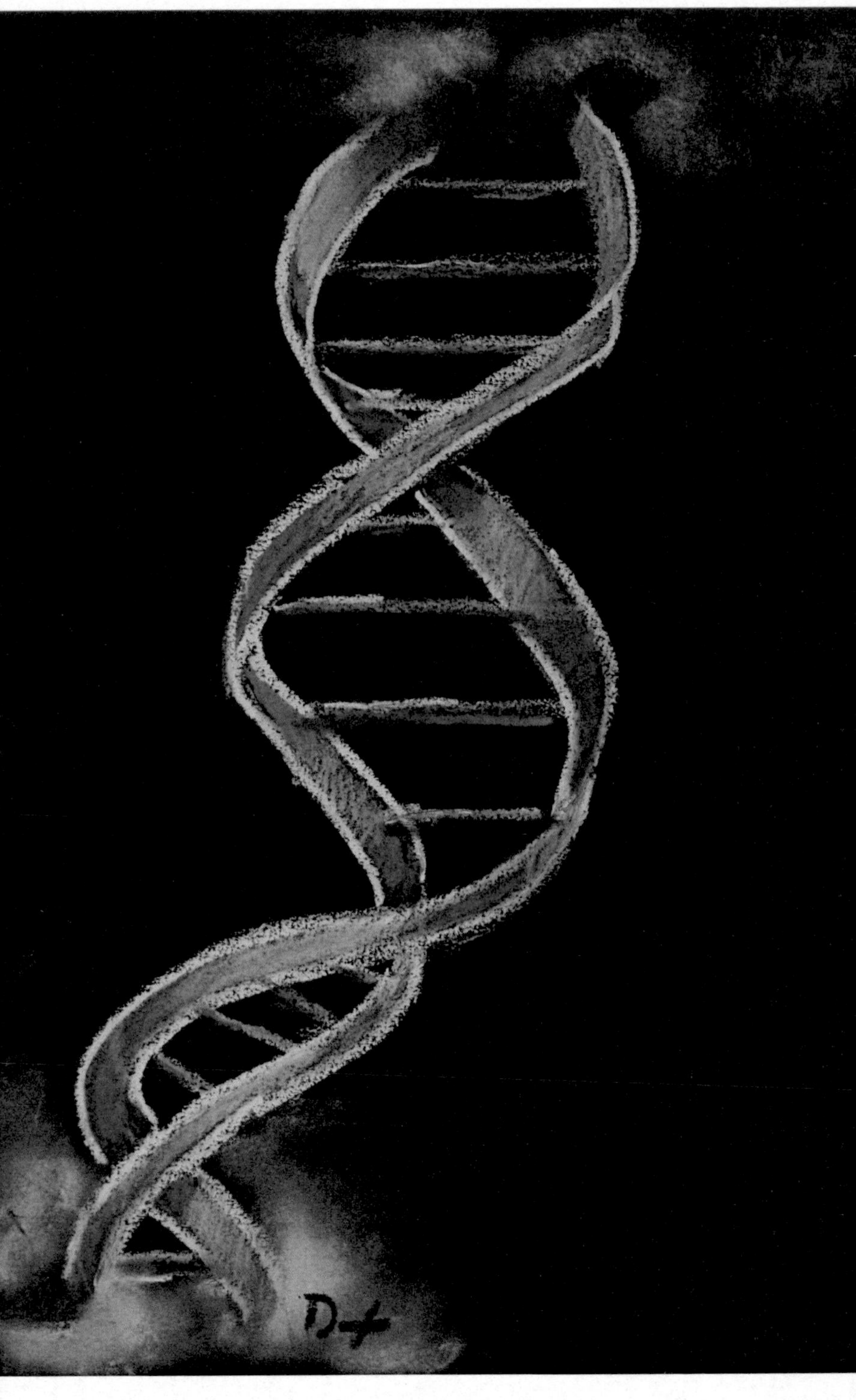

2 STUCK

My body bites the dust
day after day.
My limbs are losing motion, my spine its elasticity,
steadily my body is shedding its customs.
There are no windows in my lungs, no breeze
to break the moment,
no wormhole to some cooler galaxy.
My bed stuck in the canyon floor –
the dirt-pools in its cracks
are toxic with decay,
the plants are in a constant loop of dying,
a shrub in a frenzy of withering.

Lying here in the untiring heat,
I imagine the world falling in on itself,
hour after hour, month after month,
its desert rifts fertile with death,
its solar pulse
muscling out DNA –
perpetuum mobile
of dissolution

3 STILL-LIFE

The sun has stripped the plants bare, burnt away the clouds.
A bearded eagle hunches on a rock, sunk deep in its coat.
Nothing looms beyond this desert, where the hours shrivel,
the heat's dense hands pressing down on me.
My senses have clarity, take stock of motion's absence,
note sand-slide in tissue, heart-muscle marking time,
cells emptied of sap and oxygen,
and death a slow reprocessing, wizening of flesh.

Somewhere in this place that knows no seasons,
somewhere among rocks and dust, beyond anticipation,
a cool wind will start shifting earth, moisten the sky,
allow a root to sprout, a shoot to scramble through.
Somewhere maybe a swallow in my bones
will make its way across a border zone

4 YOU

When you entered the picture,
weaving your tales of newness,
I didn't expect you to stick around.
I thought you'd mind
stepping so close to the earth, to this rocky body,
flirting with the inorganic.

You weren't all that fazed.
Hardwired in your genome was a notion of survival,
and you seemed optimistic about canyons,
as if we were tourists here,
en route to something.

You got down to the bone of me
and I can't undo you.

But you have recovery agendas,
your eyes scan the walls for rope ladders,
while the canyon counts its wrinkles.
It has nothing to offer but itself,
there's no remedy for it

5 TOO EARLY

I woke up too early from a dream,
my dog Yoe-ti still dozing at my feet, her sleep unbroken.

I had been out walking with Yoe-ti,
she was wearing a green hat
and was always a few steps ahead of me.

Slowly the path climbed out of the canyon
to a wide sheet of sand.
The sun had perched its eye on the horizon.
I couldn't tell if it was setting or rising.

Somewhere between yet and not yet
the ground began to warp, buckling my bones,
binding my limbs to a new body-language,
and a raging hound appeared, baring its teeth.

'I am not for you,' I shouted,
bracing myself to fight

6 DAYTIME NIGHTMARE

Today there was nothing I could do.
My limbs needed that nothing, my muscles craved stillness,
my mind wanted silence, my eyes the lights out,
my skin to shed its colour
the way a tree sheds its leaves, the way the nights
want the cold.

The dust is settling on me,
there's no stopping it.

What if you let it, you said.
What if you let it in, this deadness,
that seems to insist
you let it in,
let grit cover your feet, rockfall enter your blood,
soil fill up your pores, your lungs –

so I let it.
I waited, panicked, let it.
I watched
as the sand buried me,
my bones turned brittle,
turned to dust

till I was nothing but earth,
the calm earth that the rain fell on

and something came living through that,
a few sprouting, intractable things

7 NADIR

'In my dream I saw animals sculpted along the top of the canyon, and
I was glad to be there. I felt I had discovered myth.' – Ditty Doornbos

There's nowhere else to go. This sandstone chasm
I've fallen into.

We talked about children today,
but it's too late, my ovaries are desert-dry.
Nothing will grow from me now.

Then I was deep down in the canyon again,
a lion had eaten itself into me,
from my hollows it emerged,
scaled the canyon walls and sank its feet into the cliffs
high up on a ledge.
There was nothing of illness about it.

And I saw a wolf there too, and a winged tiger,
carved in the rock-face above me.
And I walked through the depths of the canyon
while they watched over me.

I have to draw them
into this morning's daylight,
I'll keep drawing them,
digging them up from the drought of myself,

my guardians,
totems,
older than illness

8 WALKING

Every day I take a few steps along the canyon floor.
Back and forth, back and forth, so I know exactly where I am.
I must placate the nervous jinn perched on my shoulder
screaming danger
at every unfamiliar crack in the rock, every stone to stumble over.
I live close to the danger zone, but the danger zone is shifting
just beyond my furthest reach, just beyond the growing space
I am reclaiming and must not overstep.

I need to know where I am.

But I can be in the unknown.
My body is already
the unknown,
that other space called desert,
the earth I am equal to.

I'm growing equal to the earth.

Joy is the tantalising next rock formation,
the curve in the canyon with its deflected vistas,
a glimpse of early earth,
and the fact that I am wearing out my shoes

9 LOVE

If there can still be love here, after all this shedding,
if our bodies, with their bent towards erosion,
still have the knack for love,

then let's call it the embrace of the earth, this love,
where we can almost
abstract ourselves
into scree, sandstone, our carbon beginnings.

Let this love be as inescapable as the desert,
let the rifts be real and spoken about,
let my fears and yours reverse themselves
into the careless canyon,
into a chasm of solace

and leave us rooted in its indifference

10 RELAPSE

There is absolutely no way out.
I was clambering up rocks battered down by sand.
I was climbing up from the depths,
past golden thistle and thorn bush,
fingering dark shale and brighter limestone,
clawing my way to new chapters of rock,
but I keep sliding back
to the oldest tales,
when the earth was uncertain,
when tectonic plates were rent apart
and the landscape split open

11 THE OLDEST DREAM

It was the oldest night,
which was the time between old and new.
At the bottom of the canyon lived an orca –
it had swum to the depths of the earth.
On the face of the deep were other orcas,
drawing a first circle and departing.

On the second night
the first uncertainty stirred in the soil
and burrowing out came an angry mole.
I tried to put it on a leash,
but it became ungovernable.
So I let it go back underground,
to busy itself with worms.

On the third night
a bear the size of the sky wanted my blood.
There was nowhere to hide, so I didn't
and it sat down beside me, and wasn't.

On the fourth night
generations of mammoths
walked the length of the canyon
and I went from dead to mortal a hundred times.

The fifth night engendered a camel
that carried me to shelter from the wind,
the sand was stinging its eyes,
so I sheltered them with my hands.

On the sixth night
I saw a young goat on the edge of an abyss.
I tried to stop its sacrifice,
but it dived in of its own accord
and came out a white doe.

On the seventh night
a flash flood tore through the canyon,
flung me high up into the air
and onto dry land.

When I looked back, there was nowhere left to go,
so I started walking towards the unreachable distance

12 THRESHOLD

Embarking on a first small project
brings me to the threshold of your world.
I've started illustrating someone else's story,
scared my drawings are out of step,
scared of your space of deadlines and demands,
where what the mind prompts
becomes an undertaking
and instinct craves action, a leap of faith.

Out of the tangled limits
that have kept me in a place of silence,
where time refused to budge
and the heat locked me in its grip,
imprisoning and swaying
in menace and comfort,

I am catapulted
(grubby with doubt, smelling of despair)
towards your mesmerising world –

the risk of promises

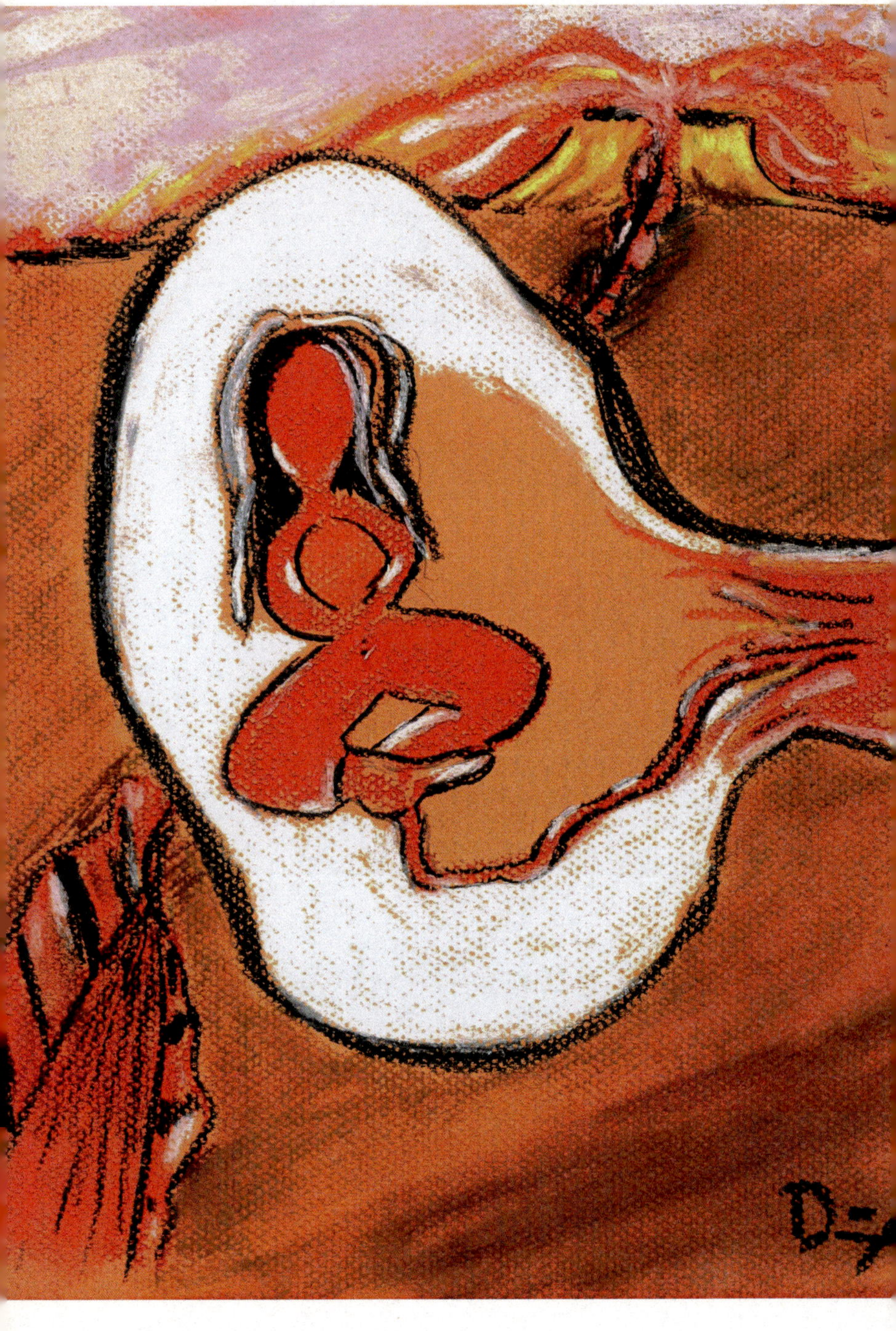

13 STAYING

I can't quite work out what we're doing yet,
but we seem to be making a life here,
in this unmythical corner of Flanders,
improvising our own rituals, tending our vegetables,
fussing over the sturgeons in the pond
we inherited from the last tenant.

I've taken in a stray dog, Lady,
because she looks just like the hound from my dream,
macabre enough for fiction, I tell you, and you grin.

The woods here are not as generous as the desert,
but on good days my walks seem endless,
with an ageing Yoe-ti limping behind me.

Earthquakes have no labour here,
the nightmares have cantered off to other pastures
and rainbows span ordinary skies.

Most days I'm at my drawing table,
learning to trust the blank page's undoing.

Every morning the sun rises
in plainest alchemy.

Only my body pre-dates itself from time to time
to a jittery shadow
the canyon stays

Judith Wilkinson, born in 1959, is a British poet and translator, living in Groningen, the Netherlands. She has won many awards for her work. In 2011 she won the Popescu Prize for European poetry in translation for her translation of Toon Tellegen's *Raptors* (Carcanet Press) and in 2013 she won the Brockway Prize. A collection of her own poems, *Tightrope Dancer*, was published by Shoestring Press in 2010. She has M.E. (also known as Chronic Fatigue Syndrome) and between 1994 and 2006 was unable to work. Her website can be visited at www.judithwilkinson.net.

Ditty Doornbos, born in 1969, is a Dutch artist and illustrator, born in Groningen, the Netherlands. She now lives in Kortessem, Belgium, with her husband Patrick and their two dogs, Yoe-ti and Lady. Doornbos and her husband recently set up their own radio station, www.radioniels.be, and host various music programmes. During her years of severe chronic illness (M.E., also known as Chronic Fatigue Syndrome) Doornbos was unable to work, but she kept a journal of her experiences and tried to capture her vivid and often mythological dreams in drawings and paintings.